I0201307

BALD CATS AND DEAF ELEPHANTS

A Book of Poetry

By: Jef Huntsman

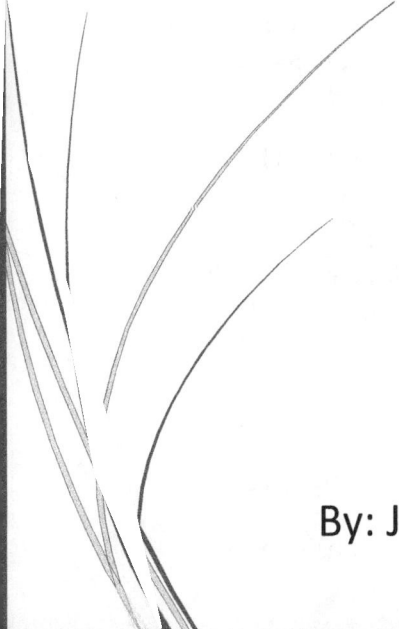

This book of poetry, and all characters contained herein are fiction. Any resemblance to actual people or real events is unintended. The places found in these pages are real with some adjustment to make them fit within the story. Any liberties taken are those of the author.

Copyright © 2018 by Jef R. Huntsman

All rights reserved. This book, or parts thereof, may not be reproduced in any form without permission.

BALD CATS AND DEAF ELEPHANTS/ Jef Huntsman – First Edition
ISBN # 978-0-9975748-4-5 (pb)
ISBN # 978-0-9975748-5-2 (ebook)

Belray Books, LLC.

Acknowledgements

Thanks to all those inspirational people at the Bards
and Scribes for all they do.
And to the League of Utah Writers who have
boosted my appreciation of writing to the
highest level.

Also, by the Author,

Jef Huntsman:

Heart Attack, Yak, Yak

Tattered Portrait

JAMAICA RUSH

Coming in the Fall, 2018

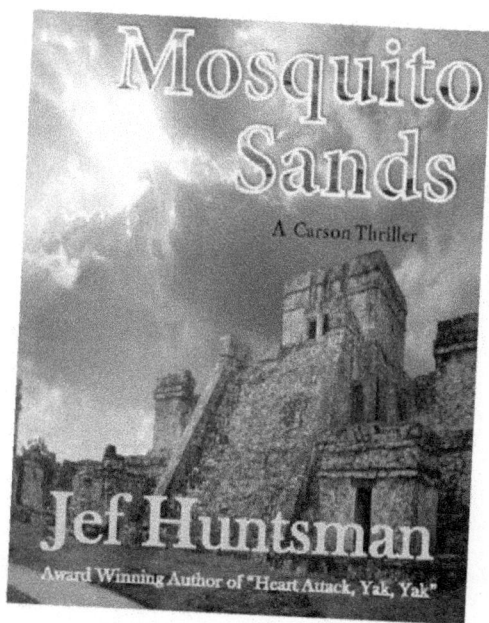

A Carson Thriller

Belray Books, LLC

Coming in the Fall 2018

WHITE ASPEN

Arise stately aspen
reach for the April skies.
The forest is hidden
with silent wooded lives.

Bark carved with devotion
expands in seasoned time.
Changed by spring's past grace.
Memories of sharper lines.

The couple searches trunks
in bouncy, giddy steps.
Eyes find the inscription,
which they blissfully left.

Pounding hearts remind them
of a much younger time.
Both for stately aspen,
and for love, now refined.

Jef Huntsman

The Feral Cat

I wish I didn't have a cat,
fierce furry rat.
The ruffle of thick feral fur,
I hear it purr.

Yellow teeth flare from cheeks, so fat.
Paws claw the mat.
My vulnerability sensed,
air between, tense.

Wild eyes glow, like burning coals,
dim like lost souls.
Hair stands up, it arches its back,
bared claws so black.

Devil's kitten revealed to sight,
I grab a knife,
determined to protect my life.
My wife walks in.

The cat me'ows, soft, without sin.
Loving arched back,
cuddles my wife, causing a laugh.
Affection bright,
hazel eyes glance down with delight.

I hide the knife,
slowly, unnoticed by my wife.
The feral cat
slyly glares at me and winks. Brat!

SNOW MELT

Warmth and rain
    melt snow up high.
Underneath
    the branches sigh.

Spring enters
    as winter complies.
Clouds open
    a view of sky.

Rivers rise
    to fill the lakes.
The song, the sound,
    the rush awakes.

Lawns watered
    buds spring forth.
Leaves unfurl
    in silent birth.

Seeds divide
    and nature sings.
Dance of birth
    of verdant things.

A KNOT UPON MY HEAD

I had a little knot
upon my hairless head.
It chattered most incessantly
while I tried to sleep in bed.

I pulled the pillow tight
against this knot so rare.
It squirmed, and throbbed, and kicked,
bucking like a wild west mare.

I tried to smack it senseless,
hitting the knot named Funk.
It prattled on and on,
I beat myself half-drunk.

By morning I was weary,
my skull in grave distress.
Funk just kept on talking,
no end to this, I guess.

I took a lovely shower
to drown the biting voice.
Palms hard against my ears,
I had no other choice.

Bald Cats and Deaf Elephants

I thought of an old tune,
and hummed with all my might.
Funk sang the very words.
Damn, he knew them, alright.
I ran my head at the fridge,
to stop this awful chatter.
I went out cold, then awoke.
It really hadn't mattered.

Constant rant, rapid chit-chat,
my mind, it was a failing.
Totally hate this knot,
no end to his constant wailing.

So, I got out my pistol,
my hand pointed the gun.
I pointed at the voice,
and then it was all done.

Jef Huntsman

Night Horse

Hooves thump solid,
swirling dust stirs.
Knees ever bending,
her stride outstretched.

Earth is gobbled,
branches quickly snapped.
Tense legs gallop,
rivers of sweat.

Rippling black muscles,
leap over logs.
Fly though the pine,
tail flowing behind.

Over the top,
a far reach out.
She thunders downhill.
Through blackened night.

Fear of attack,
horse with no rider.
Lion winded,
stops on a rock.

Horse surges forward,
blood stinging veins.
Miles blast under,
beneath thick black mane.

Horse hooves clacking,
line of the sun,
breaks night into day.
Burning lungs hurt.

Pace starts to slow,
now a cautious trot.
At water's edge,
smell silent air.

Relief blooms, safety.

Jef Huntsman

A Good Day

I want to run
I want to dance
And sing a song
And make romance.

To fill my lungs
With precious air,
Do something nuts,
Take the dare.

Ride a skateboard,
Swim in the sea.
I'd be so glad
As glad can be.

Smell a flower,
Climb up a wall,
Plant a pear tree,
Go to the mall.
I want to do most everything.
But most of all,
I want to run
    And dance
    nd sing.

OUT SLIPS MY THUMB

Under a Russian olive tree
suitcase in the grass.
Nowhere to be though.
Too much time sittin' on my ass.

Traffics a flowing.
The winds circling the mountain rim.
Eyeballing a tire shell
as it jumps in a spin.

Just me and my street pup.
We've seen most all things.
Dark cities, full of creeps in line,
unlocked doors, and stolen rings

Got nobody, but a mutt half-blind.
She has me, and I have her.
Nothing bad happenin' so far today.
My hand rolls softly over matted fur.

A bag of chips, a tilt loose mind.
Sittin', waitin', for night to fall.
Travel trailer, loaded semi,
everything else in a stall.

Evening hits and grey abounds.
Lift up suitcase, toss the rum,
grab the dog, old knees creakin'
and out slips my thumb.

The Writer

Pen keeps a scribblin'
    Paper a fillin'
Heart is a poundin'
    Fingers a crampin'
I am a willin'
    Keep on a tellin'
Stiffness is settin'
    Fingers are achin'.
Mind overpowerin'
    Pages are stackin'
Write 'til it's hurtin'
    Words never endin'
Chapters finishin'
    Pages expandin'
Oh, never endin'
    Never finishin'
Pen keeps a scribblin'
    Paper a fillin'

A Walk in the Rain

I'm angry.
Mad as hell.
This soothing rain
Is washing away
The fury deep within.
I take my steps
To nowhere fast.
Water drenching down.
Draining all the rage,
Sliding it to the ground
It's wrecked my anger fully.
Cooled the fire within.
Ruined a perfect tantrum.
Calmed a body
So worked up.
I try to anchor
The indignation
To boil it up again.
The rain never ceases
To soothe the angst within.

Jef Huntsman

THE WIND IS THE MASTER

Shifting of air
Branches bow in despair
  White caps fling
  Across the open beam
Sands curl
Grains of fury hurl
  Snow dispenses
  Clambering against fences
Clouds race
At a thinning pace
  Heads tuck
  Inside they duck

The wind is the master
With life and disaster.

THE DANCER

Pain held, deep breath.
Elastic motion begins.
      A sweeping, dawn tide.
      Air—softly touched.
The fluid, the grace.
The rise and the fall.
      Swirl of an arm.
      Twist, balanced on toe.
A delicate thunder.
Rapture of soul.
      Lunge of liquid.
      Diaphanous dignity and lithe
Perfection, as a spin unfolds.
Wood slats give slightly.
      Pain held away.
      Muscles contract.
Skin sparkles sweat.
Gravity disarmed.
      A tingle slowly
      Through my chest.
The curtain closed.
Flowers at rest.

Feud of the Towels

I wish I was a towel
A hanging on a hook.
With others of my kind
Like pages of a book.

I want to reign up high
Above Italian tile.
So dry and colorful,
Showing a pleasing smile.

No! I'm just a washcloth
Laid filthy on a rock
Frayed and tattered edges
Moldy junkyard sock.

Towel! I want to be
Sunning on snow white sand.
The breeze and ocean's hum.
The sound of island band.

No!, I'm just a washcloth.
Homeless as my master.
Wipes teeth upon my threads,
Jungle of disaster.

Life in five-star hotels
Curled white, straight lines a-fold.
Radiant aroma,
Stacked on a shelf of gold

Oh no, I see another one.
A crimson red that looks so new.
Is laying in my master's hand
He glares at me with great distaste
And walks away with red so grand.

HOMONYMIUM

Striking picture, I'd like to buy,
A pine forest with fawn and doe.
Sadly, I turn and say good-bye,
My wallet missing needed dough.
I look back, but then walk on by.

The horrid smell of smoky scents,
Puff out from a dastardly flue.
Quickly I turn, it's just good sense
But it makes me sick, like the flu.
I need pills, but I just have cents,
Damn, though to the bathroom I flew.

Heaving, I hurt my spinal cord.
It brings me down and makes me cite
A song with swear words in its chord.
As I limp slowly from that site,
I slip on a pear that's been cored.
But looking up, what a fine sight!

High in the sky, a hawk who preys,
The sun shines warm on rich and poor.
Thoughts of my Dad, a man who prays
Who taught love throughout every pore.
Humbled, I give God some due praise,
And think of his words, as tears pour

MARS

I want to have a telescope.
A telescope so grand.
That I could watch the Martians
As they crawled upon their land.
I'd spy on them as they ate lunch
At the edge of a barren sea.
Oh, I'd watch them,
I would watch them so
Until they spied
Right back at me.

THE REUNION

With frazzled hair
and cocaine teeth,
She jittered behind a torn screen door.

Her skull pronounced,
skin hung pallid,
clothes like tousled laundry.

I watched her lips
Converse with air,
with no one inside to answer.

Opened the screen,
a vacant stare,
light of distant knowing.

Her bat-like arms
reached out to me.
Pulled close to ease her sudden fear.

"Hi," she whispered.
Her raspy voice,
cracked lips devoid of expression.

Cheeks curled upward
into a smile,
as my pulse raised with love.

"Hey sis."
I kissed her head as
we embraced with childhood dreams.

THE WASP Or DR SUESS GOES CAMPING

Twinkle, twinkle
Tweedled dee
I'm petrified to finish my pee.

A wasp crawled up my special spout.
It might have left
but I have a doubt.

I dare not move.
Wait, and wait with my zipper down.
That wasp must sometime come around.

My hands are shaking.
My head drips sweat
Thoughts swarm of a safety net.

I truly thought camping was so fun.
Until that creature
disappeared from the sun.

I stand and wait–all aflutter.
Hoping there isn't
nesting in my gutter.

A scream for help
to friends nearby
sounds like a whimper, or even a sigh.

I wait all day and through the night.
My body weak,
drained of all its might.

I gently bounce up and down.
Nothing happens.
Not a sound.

By noon I hear a faint, laughing glee.
Hiking ladies step out.
Under the branch of a tree.

They all shriek and stare.
Point, with disgust
rising in the air.

One throws a rock.
The other ones follow.
Clunks on my manhood sounds quite hollow.

A wasp crawls out and flies away.
Then another, and another
until twelve made their way.

The ladies scrambled
as the wasps streamed out.
I heard myself sigh after my two-day bout.

Jef Huntsman

I love nature.
I love it so much.
But I'm using a bathroom: mirror, sink, and such.

Twinkle, twinkle
Tweedled dee
Scared forever, afraid to pee.

I want to be . . .

The Sun is a happy fellow.
He sleeps throughout the night.
Rises first and smiles,
to greet dawns early light.

I never see him up too late.
His eyes they glow a bright.
He lengthens all the shadows
along his awesome flight.

Peeking through my windows
he glistens up the dust.
And follows the same path
as if ever, he must.

I want to be a sun.
A sun would be so right.
To flavor all the beaches,
and kiss the moon goodnight.

Jef Huntsman

Cycle

Deep beneath a
grassy mound.
   An earthen hole,
   my surround
Sleeping, seeping
in the ground.
   The cycle spins.
   Circling down.
Deathly silence
never a sound.
   Barely missed?
   Never renowned
Invisible life,
less than a hound.
   Chemicals
      dispensing
        all
         around
       .

Poem for Poe

Once upon my trailer trove,
I tossed overdue bills into the stove.
Dirty dishes askew in miasmic slush
I hadn't eaten, so, what's the rush?
The wind and a branch from a dead apple tree
Scraped hard on the tin of that roof by the sea.
Me and my gerbil, hungered and cold,
He on his wheel, me, a blanket rolled.
The door lay askance in its un-firm dockin'
Old sticker proclaimin', trailer rockin' and
knockin.'
Silence ran deep, the sand lay asleep
When I and my gerbil heard a constant peck of
beak.
Through skylight blurred yellow and scratched,
We knew from whence the noise it matched.
A bird, a woodpecker, all meanness within,
Hacked at the plastic, bent tin down on the trim.
My heart was a flutter, our eyes rattled weary.
Sliver of styrene hit my cheek, I moved teary.
The red hatted bird with war laced wings,
Rat-a-tat-tatted through plastic and screen.
My gerbil and I, we hung on for dear life
The pecker was persistent, just like my ex-wife.
Finally, a head popped through with a glare.
I'm afraid me and my gerbil, wetted our underwear.

BLAME

Oh, poor me, I've lost my way.
Someone, somewhere has to pay.
I've strayed because of someone else.
Those terrible people, never myself.
I've done these horrid things you see.
It's someone's fault, but never me.
They need to cease their ways right now.
It causes me this pain somehow.
They'll never change at forcing me.
It's always, always, he or she.

BLISS

Face aglow
Sunlight caress
Shoulders back
Rising chest
Tickle spreads
Surging veins
Piano music
Happy tune
Bouncy step
Dog greeter
Cats to pet
Worry free
Bursting pride
Anticipation
First date
They meet
Halfway
Perfect mate.

BALD CATS AND DEAF ELEPHANTS – 1

Across the sky an elephant rose
His eyes bound up in white.
A fox, a Ferris wheel, two old frogs
Crept by with sheer delight.

Tiger cuddles three tiny frosted cubs.
Panther chases its tail.
Monkeys swing from dangling stars on high.
Lion paws at a devil.

The animals strolled in gay affair
We sat upon a knoll
Mom's hand held mine as we gazed above
Heaven's circus enlightened our soul.

TO THE BRIM

The liquid of your presence dear
Engulfs me, churns me, without fear.
Rushing waters, moons tide of love.
Cuddle, soothe me, like a winter glove.
Glistened tide ebbs then burst forth.
Sweet surf, curls up, magnetic north.
I feel my cup splashing over
Power surge, floating calm, take over.
You wash my soul in glittered splurge.
A gulp, a fullness, we converge.
The rhapsody of sweet adore
Each day, always, my life wants more.

Jef Huntsman

FRIEND ME!

Searching all the airways in our low
For all the friends we do not know.
Keys tapping to a song.
Nothing seems to be too wrong.

Make a comment, feel the pride.
Nothing bottled up inside.
Wondering why they would think that.
On the keyboard having a spat.

Here's my photo on the screen
Being silly, playful, mean.
Can't stop punching in my thoughts.
A millipede with endless watts.

The goal is out there: gather pals.
Collecting men, boys, girls, and gals.
List grows frantic, all aflutter.
A dancing monarch in endless butter.

Searching friends throughout the night.
Some are funny, some a fright.
Internet buddies working as one.
The hive expands we're never done.

INSPIRED YOUTH

If day was night and night was day
Would Beth, perhaps, want to play?

If I was tall and Grant was small.
When I hit him, would he bawl?

If brightness gave me all it could,
Would math be understood?

If Dad was Mom and Mom was Dad,
Does that mean I'd be only half-bad?

I also wonder if the school burned down.
Would I need to know about a noun?

These are things that puzzle me.
The teacher say's, I'm crazy
as can be.

GROWLING TOILET

I thought I had some time.
I thought I needed space.
So, I sat upon the toilet,
Leaving the whole rat race.

Feeling relaxed and calm,
My mind a floating on.
I flushed that heavenly toilet,
Sighed deeply on the john.

The toilet began to rumble,
To bellow as if cursed.
It sucked me in, legs folded
Yanked through the pipes, butt first.

My toes and hands above my head,
My back curled around a bend.
I slid through at such a speed,
I wouldn't recommend.

We popped into the sewer—
Paper, vile-slush, and me.
With quite a jolt on my ankle,
Dislocated my knee.

I'm not quite sure what the reason.
I'm not sure what I did.
But I heard a fading laugh,
From that bowl with the oval lid.

MY OWN WAY

Am I going to Heaven?
or am I headed for Hell?
Wondering, searching my life,
I truly cannot tell.

A bundle of checks in good.
But the same amount in bad.
Quite a scary destiny,
I think that I've been had.

"You haven't much time right now,"
The sad doctor proclaimed.
I'm now thinking really hard
to turn this thing one way.

I change my ways to goodness.
My mind souring perfect, pure.
I give thanks and pray and such.
Altered things—I'm pretty sure.

Second visit to my Doc
He now says, I'm just fine.
I curse, drink and carry on.
That's really my own way.

Jef Huntsman

A Novice Appraises Depression

The sink is clogged,
The dog unfed.
I'm padding off to bed.

Despair is tight
In every cell.
My body begs to fail.

The curtains shut,
Light bill unpaid.
From this I cease to wade.

Wrinkly-skin baths,
Don't make me clean.
Mind dust will never gleam.

The sun tries hard
Peaks in my room
Tight lids enjoy the doom.

The door opens.
Small children stare.
Sheets wadded worn bare.

I pray for death
With all my might.
ut, death escapes each night.

It walks on by
Spits at my ways.
Saying, I have no right
To take my life away.

DIMPLE ON MY FOREHEAD

There's a dimple on my forehead,
where the bullet passed right through.
And they say there's nothing wrong,
and they say it's nothing new.
But, I cannot zip my coat;
my brain rolls around like stew.

There's a dimple on my forehead,
and I'm not sure what to do.
I visited my doctor;
he says I'm doing just fine.
But I don't quite believe him;
I'm afraid it's just a line.

There's a dimple on my forehead,
where the bullet passed right through.
I didn't see it coming;
yes, the hole is something new.
The bullet came so quickly;
there was no one there to sue.

There's a dimple on my forehead,
perhaps help is overdue.
I walk in a grocery store,
grab the mike and start to sing.
I listen to registers
as they brightly ring and ring.

There's a dimple on my forehead,
circled in a lovely blue.
With a finger in the front
and another in the rear,
A new world opens to me;
everything becomes so clear.

There's a dimple on my forehead,
that leaks a bit of pink goo.
I see me before the hole,
before the grocery singing,
My back arched, my face forlorn,
my chin downturned and leaning.

There's a dimple on my forehead,
where the bullet passed right through.
I pull my fingers back out
and go about my day.
Everything is so pleasant.
I truly like it this way.

There's a dimple on my forehead,
where the bullet passed right through.

Jef Huntsman

Season

There's no rhyme or no reason.
When you don't have a season.
Snowflakes cannot fall from the sky.
Colorful leaves dropping don't comply.
Heat reaches up to one "0" five.
The system makes you feel so alive.
Sleighs gliding freely down a hill.
Blue birds singing on a window sill.
Growing vegetables for that time.
Hills changing to crimson, orange and lime.
Nothing better, put on a sweater.
The rain down your neck getting wetter.
When you don't have a season.
There's no rhyme or no reason.

Merry Christmas

Christmas is here.
        Oh, what a delight.
Credit cards battered,
Wallet filled with dust mites

The reindeer have messed
        On my carpet with glee.
Yanked that sleigh,
        Knocked over a tree.

The lights are all busted
        And caused quite a flame.
Firemen drenched the house.
        There's no one to blame.

The water it froze.
        My front rooms a rink.
Neighbors dropped over,
        With skates, blue and pink.

The madhouse continued,
        Those skaters and me.
Till little John fell
        And broke his wee knee.

Jef Huntsman

The lawsuits not bad.
      They're taking the house.
A widower across the street
      Moved in with my spouse.

I have a nice box.
      Not warm, but it's clean.
With little to eat
      I've gotten quite lean.

My three-wheeled shopping cart
      Scuttles along perfectly fine.
And the goiter that's growing
      Seems, it's only benign

My uncle Fred died.
      A change in my luck.
He left me a fortune.
      I'm out of this muck.

LIVIN' THE LIFE

Reading a long book,
Can't quite find the hook.
There's a smell—of swirling camp fire.
Listening to the river, digging at a sliver.
Checking a hawk,
Hunting high from a wire

So much to do, but I'll kick off my shoes.
I'm loving this beautiful day.
Course I've had a lot lately,
Half-smile, half frown is my way

I really don't know why.
She could have said goodbye?
I leaned back on my porch and waved her away.
Two swallows dart, don't think they part.
They swoop and fly
And enjoy all the day.

I'll visit Uncle Clive;
Wonder if he's alive.
Lean back as the dust blows in.
Can't put the book down, my lips just pull a frown.
Still on page five,
Toss the book in the bin

Jef Huntsman

So much to do but kick off my shoes.
I'm loving this beautiful day off.
Course I've had a lot lately.
Probably time to fill the cows' trough.
Yeah, there's time to fill the cows' trough.

FIRST SIGNS

Fling of icy waters seep,
into the ground of dead leaves deep.
Rushing down the mountain slope,
like never ending vines of rope.
Loose rock and dirt move away,
gravity flows leading the way.
Rising lakes from summer drought,
sailing ships start venturing out.
Nature smiles, full of glee,
forceful water moves out to sea.
Fish soon lose their winter still,
Pump of their blood, flash of quick tail.
Herds graze in lower terrain,
spring is coming with all its fame.
Bud's follow the sun ripe scent,
branches rise from winter long bent.
Birds to wires singing, cling,
living breathing, presence of spring.

DAD

I wish you'd seen my wedding day
And held my children's hands.
Saw their skipping with a rope
Or trying out for the band.
And kicking in a goal or two,
Picking up a fumble.
Watch their grin on Christmas morn
And heard their skateboards rumble.
You haven't met my wife, so grand,
Or heard her witty charm.
Tasted my tortilla soup,
And saw the man you have born.
For you to be as proud as I
Of what you taught to me.
I shed sweet tears for those few years
To lose a Dad so early.

The Caterpillar

I wish I had a caterpillar,
To crawl upon my knee
And talk, and talk, and talk, and talk
Telling me what she hoped to see.

She is going to be a butterfly,
A monarch, oh so grand.
She'll fly over verdant forests,
Across beaches of snow-white sand.

She might just sail the ocean so blue,
And swirl around and round.
Then she'll gently still her motion,
And flit away without a sound.

She could spot Frances' Eifel tower
From way above the Seine.
See Italy's timeless ruins
Where fierce beasts often fought with men.

I can almost hear her wings beat now,
Fluttering by the coast.
With rise and swirl on air drafts high,
Burst forth and reach the stars, almost.

Jef Huntsman

But now she's just a caterpillar
Crawling up branches new.
Feasting on leaves so bright and green,
To make her distant dreams come true.

THE NEST

The tower beckoned
Quick steps, they ascend
Two lover's hearts
Barely just friends
     A spiral of fury
     Anticipation excites
     One hand leads another
     Triumph at the top delights
Stars glistening from above
Slivered moon in motionless swath
Two lovers so breathless
Climbing steeped in sin's path.
     The passion is in haste
     The old tower creeks
     No mattress, no bed,
     No fine silk sheets
The hustle, the bustle
On spattered oak floor
They finish together
Then descend to the door.

     They part, fingers slide
     After bow of minuet
     Short black skirt
     White, muddled, and wet

Jef Huntsman

The pigeons return
To the tower, their home
Paint up the floorboards
Where wood through is shown.

WORDS

There are words
That curl your lips.
Others softly
Lump your throat.

Ones that grow euphoric.
Words with muscle might.
Some that are a touch too vain.
Others meek and mild.

But I love the live ones
That kick my brain in drive.
With focus on each syllable
Crawl upon my skin.

The words that
Take me sailing
And flying through
Stars so big and bright.

The ones pumping
Thick red blood.
And catch my breath
To flee or fight.

Jef Huntsman

To travel to uncertain times,
I wouldn't know at all,
Expanding possibilities,
Breaking through a wall.

Words you taste.
And words you smell.
Words of touch,
Dropping me to hell.

To horizons vast
Filled with fear,
And laughter,
And suspense and tear.

I'll read until I find them all
And all make perfect sense.
Many, many books there are,
Makes me so gladly tense.

WAR

War
Steps in
Without patience
Good lives disrupted
Farmland for the taking
Destroyed ground, shamble of bricks
Holes in earth, scarred, the creeping bare
Religion ofttimes designed culprit
Mindless bombing, theft of property
All in the name of a God so kind and fair
Brave soldiers, frightened civilians,
understanding rare.
Without patience
Steps in
War

Colors

Why is white a color?
It's really none at all.
And painted black
Is so absurd
A mixed pallet so pure
We have these designations
As if one is good or bad
None of them describe the soul
The dweller who sits within.
Some are high
Some are short
Some barrel chested
Some mother breasted
Ones with hearing
Ones without
Ones who scuttle and run about
Ones who never get out.
A few that know so much indeed
A few that barely read
A few that smile with eyes so round
A few that growl and stomp the ground
A mix of colors
We display
All are good
Never take that away.

ADHD Poem

Sitting and squirming
Twisting and worming.
Don't even realize I'm moving at all.
Leg starts a thumpin'
Knee is a pumpin'.
The clock on the wall seems to forever stall.
I'm tapping my pen.
Head bobs like a hen.
The beat in my head, swift as a river bed.
Rhythm a rocking,
Switches never blocking.
Everything from cornbread to beachhead.
Teacher called my name.
Riding the brain train.
Footsteps come a calling down the aisle.
Tap on my shoulder.
Teachers gawk, full smolder.
Turn my amazed innocence to a smile.
She strolls to the front
With an annoyed grunt.
So, I'm sitting and squirming,
And twisting and worming.

Poem for a Poem

I am a poem
I can rhyme with dome
I am a poem
And sometimes I roam.
I am a poem
Even written in London or Rome
I'm still a poem
When flowing soft as foam
I'm even a poem
Shining like chrome
I even a poem
When texted on a phone
I am a poem
Spinning like a cyclone
I'm still a poem
Whether I rhyme with comb,

> Or gnome,
> Or alone.

Meeting by Chance

Elevator opens
There she stands
Smirk of love unknown
Chest blossoms
Short catches in mid-breath
Rise of an inner sigh
Enchanting describes
What she's become
Black hair, grace, style
Split second memories
Feelings I cannot hide
Ocean eyes catch mine
A fling of misplaced hair
Her brain is sifting
Long lost sun filled days
Long lost moonlit nights
She nods, face aglow
Rushes from open doors
Steps slightly on my toe
My arm is raised
For full embrace
She barrels right on by
Grabs the man
Standing quietly behind
Arms snake his neck
A lover's wrap
Of full embrace

Jef Huntsman

Ending my romance
Love slipping right on by.

Palms and Digits. poem

It swats, and slaps, and makes a fist
And gives the finger too.
My hand can bang the desk so hard
Caress a cheek adieu.

Wave hello to a friend in need.
Catch a spinning flyball.
Strum beauty on an old guitar.
Raise high for the roll call.

Towel off sweat from a wet brow.
Twist a juice lid solidly tight.
Fling a fly rod with bait and hook.
Squeeze a tin can with delight.

Shake another just like itself
Turn on lights with a switch
Plant a garden in the sunshine
Rip out weeds from a ditch

Animal shadows on the wall.
Instrument in the band.
Ink sayings on a bathroom stall.
Lead troops with firm command.

Jef Huntsman

Whittle at a piece of driftwood.
Gesture with, understood.
Sometimes a hand does greater good.
Grows big from childhood.

ALL CHANGE

Mighty sun lifts with slow embrace.
Continues to warm early frost.
Light glistens morning rivulets,
Slides across natures painted leaves.
Drips carefully with even spurts
On rotted years of autumns past.

Jef Huntsman

THE LAST DATE

I gave her three books to read.
She curtsied, smiled, and gave me a wink.
Putting them on her head,
she walked posture perfect to the sink.

LOSS IS ALWAYS THERE

Barreling down on screaming rails
The luge with gravity's pull.
We ride the edge without a care,
Pupils dilatated stare.
Grasp together like a team.
Our bodies have lost their substance.
And tears rage on 'til nothing's there.
Hope has passed a vanishing point.
Denial, anger, bargaining.
Depression flutters through space.
Acceptance is the one false thing
That never solidifies.
Holds our soul in fading embrace,
Rides down soft cloudy space.
Together the luge slid steady.
Stretch of cheeks never ending.

BLAME

Oh, poor me, I've lost my way.
Someone, somewhere has to pay.
I've strayed because of someone else.
Those terrible people, never myself.
I've done these horrid things you see.
It's someone's fault, but never me.
They need to cease their ways right now.
It causes me this pain somehow.
They'll never change at forcing me.
It's always, always, he or she.

Sudden Fear

Window taps
In pelts of rain
Do not answer
Do not blame
Only weather
Just outside
Not unknown
Nothing to hide

Coveted

Grey coat, frayed and patched
Dropped limply on small frame.
Tossed off baby carriage
Only possession to her name.
        Wind picked up, snowdrifts curled,
        The tarp her home, she huddled.
        Eyeless gaze upon her face.
        Coat tight, heart lost, so muddled.
A wad of cash, I handed her.
Grateful smile, embarrass within.
Glance at gap in heavy tarp
I stared at cheap wine sin.
        Bottles filled the carriage.
        She yanked the cover back.
        Sneer and spat words caused concern.
        Certain things, she didn't lack.

ALLOWED ONCE

By the crackers and Havarti
At a crowded, nonsense party.
        Eyes of sun, hair of wind.
        Breathless air, lungs confined.
Heart beat with sarcastic banter.
Follow her by the flower planter.
        Grabbed my elbow in a giggle.
        Freely feeling, not committal.
The swelling of sincere romance.
On the beach, we would dance.
        Electric touch of her soft hand
        As she pulled me to the sand.
Waves roared, splashed at stars.
Thinking, book of memoirs.
        The moon hung high, lovely sliver.
        While our bodies crossed to shiver.
We watched the constellations sing.
All the while, flowing air like spring.
        We never met again, I fear.
        Results as this, could not appear.

MEMORIES

Faded
Twisted
Sunlit
Folded
Shifted
Sifted
Sensual
Whittled
Forgotten
Joyful
Loving
Horrific
Tantalizing
False
Contained
Blasted
Silly
Memories

Bald Cats and Deaf Elephants – 2

Standing upon a sun-greened, plant-filled sea.
A deaf elephant who flies like a bee.

Smiling and stomping on soft mucky ground.
Squishing vegetation without much sound.

Her trunk bulbs as if it were a church bell.
Purple belly, or is that just a tale?

But she knows hundreds of rock songs by heart.
She sings to the wind, her legs firm apart.

A humming resounds across the distant shore
Where sits a bald cat, droning lull pours.

Harmonize through the day, and into the night.
 Watching them sing, always a splendid sight.

Sunrise comes, and they head separate ways.
Grin from the bald cat as she strolls away.

The deaf elephant flies across the bay.
Silent end until another day.

Jef Huntsman

Day Sleeper

The rake of sunshine
Glitters through the trees.
Breaks through depression
That buckles sturdy knees.
The warmth gives me spirit.
The light gives slight push.
But, I am like the quail,
That scatters under a bush.
I know the sun is just a friend,
And not a foe to hide.
But so much night, upon my day
Has sent me on this ride.

BEGINNING SEASON

Bare trees inhale
The light absorbed
Warming soil
Unfolding nakedness
Blooms on the exhale

Jef Huntsman

BLACK AND BLUE

I feel I'm not as nimble
As I used to be
But at least the skateboards
Still as solid as a tree

FOUR HAIKUS

The flu
        The urinal
                The doorbell rings

Leaves sit still on a grave
        Spiral up
                Paint another

Scampering mice
        My big toe
                Captured in a mouse trap

The warmth of the fire
        Spits coals
                Silence ensues

TINY PACKAGE

The whisper of a shadow near.
Brings a smile of inside cheer.
Tiny steps that beckon from behind.
Joy engulfs my playful mind.
The soft patter approaches close.
Exuberant surprise of prose.
A happy giggle, quick embrace,
The warmth of granddaughter's embrace.

SAILING

I once saw the back of a boat.
It leaned barely afloat.
The captain he climbed up the mast.
Others followed, until the last.
A crack, and all in the moat.

Jef Huntsman

MONDAY

The door to my house is askew.
The dog ripped apart my shoe.
My breakfast is black.
My jobs of great lack.
And this, my Monday, nothing new.

The Cell

Baffled, smiling hesitation
Speeds across each nation
Typing babbled communication
As if important legislation.

Our overpowering creation
Salves, sweet medication
Such strong adoration
Brings about sedation

Truly there's no cessation
Knowing our location
Scribbling, thumbing damnation
Fury of blood irrigation

We began this gestation
Is it our flotation?
Or a powerful deflation
Into self-adoration.

BIRTHDAY

My back against hard bark of a pine.
Needles spike the bottom of my skirt.
Desire of life sucked away, gone.
Toe inflamed, seepage from the hurt.

Fifteen years ago, this day
Mom gave a hard birth.
The deep shade of the tree
Darkens the price I'm worth.

Flattened candy sacks watch
As the day lingers on.
Creeps stroll by with leering eye.
My mind humming a lost song.

Tuck up legs, becoming one with the tree.
Exhale. Soft soles disappear with time.
Soiled fingers search my pockets
Find broken peanuts and a dime.

Stomach can't recall a last meal.
Plastic sack does a dance
With paper in an upward twirl.
Wind creating its own romance.

Bald Cats and Deaf Elephants

A couple holding hands
Aged, battered, and in love.
Their backs in a stoop.
Playful shoulder shove.

They notice me with smiles
Entering my curtained seclusion.
My heart slamming against skin,
Trapped in my own disillusion.

Outstretch of hand, wrinkled and spotted.
Thick roll of Jacksons, flutters like leaves.
In their eyes, a humble flame
Knowing we both gain, and receive

They walk away without a word.
The best birthday I've ever had.
Tears wiped on my tattered sleeve.
 For nameless grandma and granddad.

MILK BOMB

Flying through the torn screen door
The Milkman's nose slams to the floor.

The tray of gallons spins the air
Crashes before the kitchen chair.

Cow milk bomb slimes mom's brass.
Blankets baby in a glue-like mass.

Screech from the high stool, curls our spine.
Hands splashing tray, stopping the whine.

Dog rolls in, bites the intruders butt.
Then slides on all fours, yelping mutt.

Mom comes just out of the shower.
Curler sizzles hair to powder.

Milkman pedals air, flies into Mom.
Legs fling, the great milk tsunami.

Mom hates that my room is a mess.
Cell pics, fold arms, useful protest.

www.ingramcontent.com/pod-product-compliance
Lightning Source LLC
Chambersburg PA
CBHW021211020426
42331CB00003B/304